Passion and Freedom

A Resource for Couples

UNITED CHURCH
PUBLISHING HOUSE

Passion and Freedom: A Resource for Couples

National Library of Canada Cataloguing in Publication

Passion and freedom : a resource for couples.

Includes bibliographical references.

ISBN 1-55134-131-X

1. Church work with married people. 2. Marriage—Religious aspects—United Church of Canada.

BV4012.27.P378 2003   259'.14   C2003-907100-6

United Church Publishing House
3250 Bloor St. West, Suite 300
Toronto, ON M8X 2Y4
416-231-5931
www.united-church.ca

Cover design: Diane Renault, Graphics and Print
Inside design: Ian Ball
Cover photo: Claudia Kutchukian, Resource Coordination

Printed in Canada

5 4 3 2 1   07 06 05 04 03   030400

Contents

Part III. Middles: Compassion and Renewal 25

Part IV. Endings: Grief, Mystery, and New Beginnings 51

Appendix A. The United Church of Canada: What We Believe 63

Further Reading 65

Introduction

Purpose of This Guide

Marriage/lifelong partnership is one of the most important commitments you will make to another person. To share intimately in another's life is both a gift and a challenge. This guide has been written to offer support to you as a couple as you seek to nurture and live out your covenant relationship through the years you will share together as partners.

In producing this guide, The United Church of Canada has sought to offer support through the beginnings, middles, and endings of relationships for both heterosexual and homosexual couples. This booklet offers you some reflective prose with accompanying questions, and some exercises that we hope will help you, as a couple and as individuals, to grow in your relationship.

Spirit of This Guide

Passion is a profound word in our Christian tradition. In daily speech, it usually refers to sexual energy and wild love. Passion is the ability to feel strongly, to feel desire, love, breakage, grief, and joy. Jesus says that he has come that we might have life and have it abundantly. Passion is about being fully and *abundantly* alive, in all the pain and glory of human life. Passion is related to the word *passive*: It is not about control, but rather about facing with grace what is given in life.

Compassion means literally "to suffer with." Compassion grows out of the capacity for passion—to feel with another, as that person lives in the truth of her or his life. As followers of Jesus, we who claim the name Christian are committed to nurturing caring, compassionate, whole, and sacred relationships among all the participants in the relationship.

Freedom is the opportunity to move toward living more deeply and lovingly in the unique realities of our lives, our society, and our planet today. A covenanted, committed life relationship can be a journey together where each partner discovers, over and over, the freedom to love.

Celebrating the Holy in the Everyday

Many couples are open to finding sacredness in the midst of their everyday lives. Many couples seek to find the "more" of life, to find deeper meaning for their lives and for their relationships. Whether you have your own words for this spiritual journey, you may desire to find God, however you may call God, in the joys, struggles, transitions, and choices of your relationship.

The church can offer you and your partner valuable help with your unique dances of intimacy and anger, your communication and relationship-building skills, your attention to family of origin issues, and your awareness of your desires and dreams. This guide offers you some foundational exercises in these areas.

In addition, the church can offer you

- resources to learn to hallow relational space between you and your partner and to find your shared spiritual identity

- companionship and authenticity to the work of exploring the holiness of living together in life partnership

- a place to return to when finding sacred meaning in your life is too hard

- a friend to journey with you through the stages of your relationship and of your spiritual journey

Covenant and Marriage as a Sign[1]

In our faith tradition we understand marriage/lifelong partnership to be a covenant. It is not simply a social arrangement, a legal bond, or even a personal commitment, but a holy covenant in which God is an active partner.

Taken literally, *covenant* means simply a bond, an agreement, or a "deal" made between two parties and confirmed (sealed) by some sort of symbolic gesture—a gift, meal, handshake, kiss. In its biblical context, however, the term takes on a deeper meaning: It has to do with the promises and purposes of God. A covenant defines the fundamental relationship between God and humankind.

The biblical God is, by nature, communal and relational rather than solitary and uninvolved. God has created us for relationship, for community. Covenantal marriage/lifelong partnership is more than a private event. It involves a very public acknowledgement and celebration of a relational process that is also intensely personal, intimate, joyful, mutual, lifelong, faithful, and dynamic.

Marriage/lifelong partnership is also an interpersonal relationship. As such, it offers the promise, though certainly not the guarantee, of a very special kind of intimacy between two people, an intimacy that is characterized by deep trust and vulnerability. It involves self-revelation, shared values, laughter, tears, and space to move and grow, not only as a couple but also as individuals.

Covenantal commitment is a joyful experience. In the marriage/commit-ment ceremony we are called upon to rejoice with you in your happiness. Afterwards, we gather with you to eat and drink in joyful celebration. This is not to deny the reality that conflict and compromise will be a part of this relationship, too.

Covenantal marriage/lifelong partnership is not dominant/submissive but rather mutual and life-giving. Mutuality does not mean some kind of mechanical "equality" at every point but rather a genuinely shared responsibility for decisions and tasks, always recognizing and valuing the interests and gifts of each partner.

At its best, this relationship is a lifelong partnership of mutual love. This is not to say that the covenant cannot be broken by offence, abuse, or neglect, though the goal and intent is still for the relationship to be lifelong.

Covenantal marriage/lifelong partnership includes the expectation of fidelity. To be faithful within the "bonds" of this relationship calls for a loyalty that extends beyond the sexual—one that, in fact, includes all aspects of life together.

This partnership is dynamic, not static. It is a lifelong process of interaction and growth. As such, it will have its ups and downs, its conflicts and its resolutions, its potholes and its breakthroughs.

In marriage/lifelong partnership, God's covenantal love finds expression not in some abstract way, but in and through the promises and practices of those who open themselves to its amazing possibilities.

Structure of This Guide

This guide is divided into four parts:

- *Part I—Foundations* presents basic principles that apply to you as a couple at any stage of shared life.

- *Part II—Beginnings: Choice, Power, Vision, and Joy* offers resources for you as a couple preparing to celebrate your marriage or covenant.

- *Part III—Middles: Compassion and Renewal* helps you as a couple live out, widen, and deepen your commitment over a lifetime.

- *Part IV—Endings: Grief, Mystery, and New Beginnings* addresses the period of most radical and painful transformation of your relationship: death or divorce.

Some of the topics and exercises will be more relevant to you than others at this stage of your relationship. Use what fits and adapt what needs to be adapted.

Our Hope for You

It is our hope that you will return to this resource many times throughout the years of your relationship. It is also our hope that you will turn to the church to support you and walk with you through the joys and challenges of your relationship.

May God's deepest blessing of peace, joy, hope, and love touch your life with passion and freedom.

Family Ministries
Faith Formation and Education Unit
The United Church of Canada

Note

1. With thanks to Don Gillies for writing much of this section.

Part 1

Foundations

Chapter 1

Basic Principles for Relationships

Effective Communication

Effective two-way communication is the fundamental skill everyone needs in order to build relationships that are just, open, fulfilling, and loving. The ability to listen with understanding, acceptance, and respect is crucial to effective two-way communication. Such communication involves not only conveying thoughts and feelings through words, gestures, or behaviour, but also listening to what someone else is conveying.

Listening can be immensely difficult, especially when you don't want to hear something because it doesn't meet your own interests or desires. Yet listening is essential to a healthy, fulfilling relationship that is respectful of both partners. What is needed is a "meeting of meanings," not necessarily agreement.

Effective two-way communication includes the following, all of which can be learned and improved:

- being in touch with your feelings, hopes, dreams, expectations, roots, and influential life experiences.

- being able to express these feelings, hopes, dreams, and so on to another person in words, gestures, and behaviour.

- being able to listen to expressions of the feelings, hopes, dreams, and so on of another person without biasing such expressions with your own needs and wants, becoming defensive, debating, commenting, arguing, or blocking out, all of which indicate that you are not listening. When you listen, your comments should be intended to seek clarification or to give clues that you are listening to what is being said.

Effective communication requires

- a genuine desire to listen

- a time and place where the commitment to listen can be kept

- the ability to accept the mood and feelings of the other person

- the confidence and trust that the other person is able to handle his or her own feelings

- the ability to see and understand the other person as separate and independent from you
- respect for the other person

The one who is speaking must

- make clear, understandable statements using as many "I" messages as possible. Deal with one thought or feeling at a time.
- be honest and share her or his real feelings. This requires that a person be in touch with those feelings and own them.
- try not to settle for anything but accurate understanding of what is being expressed. Repeat the message until it is clearly understood.

The one who is listening must

- listen without comment, argument, or discussion
- listen for the feelings behind the words being spoken (empathize)
- feed back what has been heard and observed in his or her own words to check for clarity
- accept the speaker's corrections and clarifications and feed them back until the speaker is satisfied that she or he is understood
- be patient and present for the speaker, putting his or her own agenda on hold

Honouring Others' Feelings

Feelings or emotions are "gut" reactions to a situations, people, our own behaviour, or our sense of self. Feelings are neither good nor bad; they just are. However, what we do with them can be good or bad, constructive or destructive, helpful or unhelpful.

There are different levels of feelings, and often one feeling hides another. For example, anger can be a "surface" feeling that has been triggered by a deeper feeling of hurt. We have very little control over our emotions. We can deny that we are having them and cover them up, but that is not control, nor is it healthy. We do have control, however, over how we let our emotions affect us, how we express them, and how we deal with them.

When someone expresses a feeling to us, the best thing we can do is empathize—that is, accept that person's feeling and try to become aware of it ourselves. To happiness we might say, "That sounds wonderful!" To sadness we might say, "That seems pretty painful." It is not helpful to try to deny someone's feelings by saying, "Oh, you don't really feel that way," or "You shouldn't say that!" Such denials of or judgements about another's emotions may be signs that we do not wish to hear, let alone empathize, and they do nothing to change the fact that that is what the person is feeling. Again, *feelings just are.* They can be described and do not need to be justified or excused.

Personality Types

Everyone has a unique personality type that influences how they live in relationship. Personality types affect how we react to different situations and deal with different emotions. This book does not explore personality types in detail, but the exercises will help you identify features of your and your partner's personality type. We suggest that you become familiar with your personality types and how these influence your relationship.

For more information, you can visit the Web sites of the following organizations. Remember, however, that all personality tests and models have limitations and biases, and many have been criticized for being inaccurate or simplistic. These models are best seen only as tools that can help us understand more about ourselves, rather than as "answers" to who we—or other people—are.

- Myers-Briggs Type Indicator: www.myersbriggs.org
- Keirsey Temperament Sorter: www.keirsey.com
- Taylor-Johnson Temperament Analysis: www.tjta.com

Budget and Finances

Financial issues are often a source of stress for couples. In fact, financial issues rank highly as contributing factors in the failure of relationships. This book does not explore budgets and finances in detail; many books and other resources are available on these topics. In addition to referring to such resources, you can discuss with your partner the financial realities of your relationship and how to better communicate effectively with each other about them. Clarifying your core values would be an excellent place to begin. You need to understand your own and your partner's foundational values. Any differences between you over financial decisions may reflect dissonance in your basic values.

If you and your partner share a core value of mutuality, you might choose to pool your financial resources in joint bank accounts. If independence is important to both of you, you might decide to keep separate accounts, contributing to a common fund for your shared expenditures or each taking responsibility for your bills in an equitable manner.

No matter what core values are held within your relationship, money decisions involve both trust and accountability. Withholding information about money decisions implies lack of trust and is often done out of fear that a partner will disapprove of one's choices. If that is the case, the relationship is in questionable territory from the beginning due to core values that have not been adequately explored. Secrecy about how money is spent could indicate that a partner is hiding compulsive shopping, gambling, alcoholism, drug use, or payment for sex. Unexplained expenditures for restaurants, motel rooms, or gifts also obviously indicate reason for concern. Trust grows within a relationship in which there is mutual financial accountability, where there is nothing to hide.

Financial issues also relate to power in relationships. Does one of you earn substantially more than the other? Does one of you bring more investment or inherited money into the relationship than the other? How will these dynamics affect other areas of your relationship? Is the one who brings the most money into the relationship also the decision-maker, the controller of the bank account?

Second or subsequent partnerships introduce additional financial complications depending on whether children are involved. You need to make intentional decisions on whether financial responsibilities for each other's children are within or outside the scope of the relationship. This will also affect whether bank accounts are "yours and mine" or "ours."

If debt seems to be a major source of stress or conflict for the two of you, consider seeking financial advice. Bank managers can be solid sources of financial information and strategies, and do not charge for their time or advice. You might also use any credit-counselling services available in your community.

Rituals

Rituals can mark special events in your life as a couple. They involve setting aside time in your daily routine to honour the moment with symbols, actions, or words. Some rituals may be repeated many times throughout your relationship, while others may occur only once in your lives together. Take time to cherish and hold close to your heart your relationship and the moments in it that enrich and challenge you. Share them with each other and offer them to God.

Creating Sacred Space: A Sacred Cloth

Choose a cloth that you can use to create or designate a sacred space in your home and in your daily lives. The cloth can be something you buy, a handwoven piece of fabric, a scarf, a table runner, or a placemat. It can be something you already own, such as a square from a now worn-out piece of clothing that is special to both of you in some way, or a simple patchwork of several fabrics. In other words, any piece of cloth will do, but it should hold some meaning for both of you.

Hold the cloth between the two of you. Look at its threads and notice the texture, weave, and colours. Appreciate the beauty of this cloth and think of it as a symbol of your relationship—the threads, texture, colour, diversity, and strength that both of you bring to this relationship.

Place this cloth in a spot that will remind you of the richness, strength, and beauty of your relationship. If in your wedding/covenant ceremony you are or have used a "unity" candle, you may want to place this candle on your cloth as a visible reminder of the covenant you have made.

From time to time, you might make time to light the candle together, be still with each other, and remember and cherish what you each bring to your relationship.

Your Storybook

Together, begin to create a book that tells your story. Include in it pictures and reflections on the early stages of your relationship, your family trees, and information on your families of origin and the significant people and places in your lives. As you grow as a couple, add stories, pictures, and reflections of your life together.

Blessing Cup

The image of a cup is a rich one in our faith tradition. Psalm 23:5b–6 speaks of abundance and confidence: "…my cup overflows. Surely goodness and mercy shall follow me all the days of my life, and I shall dwell in the house of the Lord my whole life long."

Jesus' first miracle, at the celebration of a wedding, was to turn water into excellent wine. Then he sent a cup of the wine to be tasted by the steward of the feast. Jesus offers his followers a sacramental ritual to partake of his own Spirit, symbolically his own blood, through the shared cup of intimacy, of deepest communion. The communion bread and cup are sacramental elements that link Christians across generations, cultures, and denominations.

As a couple, find a beautiful, goblet-style cup made of pottery, metal, or glass. It can be made, found, or purchased. Keep the cup in an accessible place of honour in your home (possibly on your sacred cloth), where you will see it and use it often in simple rituals that symbolize your shared solidarity and hope. You might use the cup in a daily or weekly moment to share in each other's pain and joy in a symbolic way; in a particular moment of joy, loss, grief, transition, or fear; or for a significant anniversary.

Here's a simple structure for a blessing cup ritual. Plan ahead: Choose and have ready a drink to fill the cup, prepare a reading if you want, and set the space with a cloth, candles, or whatever marks this as a special moment for both of you.

1. Fill the cup slowly and attentively with a favourite drink.

2. Lift the cup and offer a prayer, song, or simple words—something that creates a beginning moment to name the occasion of this ritual.

3. Holding the cup between you, read something aloud that marks the moment, occasion, or anniversary. This could be a poem, a Bible passage or psalm, something inspirational from a book or letter, or a news item—something that is meaningful to both of you.

4. Sit in silence together, letting the words and moment bring your hearts to a point of quiet.

5. Give voice to something that is in your heart, and offer it as part of what fills the cup. This could be your thanksgiving, pain, fear, longings, concerns, or prayers. It could take the form of sharing your thoughts with your partner or be a personal prayer.

6. Pass the cup back and forth to each other, looking into each other's eyes and drinking all of the contents together, slowly and reverently.

7. End with a word of blessing for each other. This can be as simple as "Peace to you!" "Amen," "Thank you," or even, if you want a lighter touch, that Canadian classic, "Have a nice day!"

Part II

Beginnings:

Choice, Power, Vision, and Joy

Chapter 2

Seeking the Blessing

Wedding/Covenant Preparation

You are beginning a new stage in your relationship—you are choosing to make a public commitment to each other. At this moment you may not be thinking about a blessing: Your energies may be more focused on your florist, caterer, clothing, and family tensions. But you have decided to have a public recognition of your commitment to each other, and you have invited the church to walk with you in your public commitment.

You may be having a church wedding/covenant because that is what your family expects—but hopefully somewhere under that is a hunger for the blessing of tradition, of your ancestors, of something bigger than just the two of you. You will confer this blessing on each other, and the church will bear witness to it and seek to support you as you journey together.

In chapters 3–6, you will explore four themes central to a spirituality of lifelong partnership:

- choice
- power
- vision
- joy

Your minister will be sharing a variety of exercises on these themes with you. You may wish to insert copies of these exercises into this book, to revisit throughout the years of your relationship.

Chapter 3

Choice

Your Story

Marriage or any other covenant relationship involves a bold *choice*. You choose a partner beyond all others to make that person the focus of your strongest desires for romance, friendship, and erotic and spiritual companionship. You choose to belong to each other, to become "us"—a new relational and familial entity that carries profound social, legal, and even political implications.

Your unique story as a couple—your "story of us"—is your own personal sacred history. Learning to tell your shared story to each other and to others is fundamental to your shared spirit as a couple.

The radical call of Christian union invites each of you to leave your original family to form a new primary bond. Yet each of you also paradoxically chooses to embrace your partner's originating family and culture.

The family or community in which we grow up gives us expectations of what "normal" looks like. In choosing a partner, people take a risk, venturing into the unknown of someone else's reality. To put it simply, we all, consciously or unconsciously, see ourselves as normal and our partners as not normal. Much conflict comes from earnest efforts to assist partners in becoming "more normal."

New discoveries will continue throughout a lifetime! Maybe you won't discover until more than a decade into your covenant that your partner sees the dining-room table as a good place for kids to do their homework on, while you know tables are only for eating on. Or much later, after many decades together, you may stumble over differences of opinion about how your partner ought to behave after a major health crisis or how retirement pensions should be saved or spent. All our lives, we carry with us the norms of our first or chosen families and bear the shock of discovering alternative realities.

Some Questions to Explore as a Couple

Consider your relationship and answer these questions:

1. When and how did you meet as a couple?

2. How did you "fall in love"? Or how did you grow into love?

3. Who proposed marriage or covenanting? Where? When? How?

4. Whose story or model outside your own family of origin inspires you as you set about forming your own life partnership?

5. Why do you want to celebrate your union in church?

6. What do you dream of for your union?

7. What would you like from the minister in joining your story?

8. What arrangements have you made or hope to make for celebrating your union?

    Continue your story by working together on the exercise that follows.

Couple Dialogue

Finish each of the statements below. When you're done, take turns reading a statement aloud to your partner, and then listening to her or his version. Go back and forth, alternating between taking the lead and really listening to your partner without comment.

1. A peak experience in our relationship was _____

_____

_____.

2. I just love it when you _____

_____

_____.

3. I am proud of you when _____

_____

_____.

4. Something you have helped me learn about myself is _____

_____

_____

_____.

5. I have the most fun with you when _____

_____

_____.

6. What helps us to grow closer is _____

_____

_____.

7. One thing I regret having done is _____

_____

_____.

8. Something I find hard about you that we seldom talk about is

_____

_____.

9. An important issue between us right now is _____

    _____

    _____.

10. An area in which I would like to feel more equal with you is

    _____

    _____.

11. It really makes me mad or hurts me when you_____

    _____

    _____.

12. One thing I have always wanted to talk more about is _____

    _____

    _____.

13. The ways I like you to touch me are _____

    _____

    _____.

14. Physical affection is best for me when _____

    _____

    _____.

15. I believe in and am committed to _____

    _____

    _____.

16. I dream that together we could _____

    _____

    _____.

When you have gone through all the statements, reflect on what you
have learned from your partner, what surprised you, and what you
need to discuss in further depth. Risk being as fully open and honest as
you can.

Chapter 4

Power

Power, Conflict, and Boundaries

When you commit yourselves to be partners for the long haul, you open yourselves to grow in the sharing of *power*. Truly sharing power in a committed relationship is challenging: The principle of equal partnership affects everything from who cooks and who washes up to who pays the bills and who determines how to spend limited financial resources.

Relational conflict occurs when a person's power trespasses on another's boundaries. Conflict is an inevitable part of relationships, but the goal is to engage in healthy conflict that leads to growth and change. Conflict reminds us that something important is happening in the relationship.

Power and boundary issues are most clearly and regularly reflected in who does what in a relationship, how much control and authority are invested in those activities, and whether the power is shared relatively evenly or unevenly. Domination, submission, withdrawal, complaining or nagging, passive/aggressive behaviour, and even violence are all attempts to equalize a perceived power imbalance.

Powerlessness and Disempowerment

A person experiences *powerlessness*, or a sense of loss of control, when he feels forced to do something he does not want to do or to be someone he does not want to be. Conversely, a person feels *disempowered* when she feels blocked or prevented from doing what she wants to do. At such times, she may feel she is being denied, rejected, or devalued, and thus may feel angry, hurt, resentful, or vengeful. Committed lifelong partnership by its very nature makes new demands on each partner and puts limits on a person's desires that may be difficult or even unacceptable.

In lifelong love, occasions of unexpected power struggle and significant control issues will inevitably erupt between you and your partner. This is not a scandal! Rather, in the context of long-term love and fidelity, it is an invitation to grow beyond individual egos, to learn to engage conflict positively, to practise forgiveness, and to allow yourself to be forgiven. In the Christian life, Jesus invites his followers to move beyond themselves and engage intimately in relationships that nurture life in all its fullness. Marriage or covenant partnerships are a primary path for living out that invitation on a daily basis.

Empowerment

At their finest, Christian lovers find themselves entering and participating in a love that, rather than confining, *empowers* them. Together you will learn mutual self-giving and receiving and to plan, envision, and grow together. In partnership, you build something new and wondrous beyond what either of you could have individually accomplished or imagined.

Some Questions to Explore as a Couple

Reflect on power and conflict in your relationship:

1. How would you describe the power balance in your relationship as it relates to decisions about

   * purchases?
   * choices of holidays?
   * time spent with family?
   * other areas?

2. Describe what happens when you face times of conflict (e.g., raise your voice, stomp off, cry).

3. How do you know your opinion is heard/valued by your partner?

4. When you feel angry, how do you express your anger?

5. Do you see yourselves working as a team? If so, how?

   Continue your story by working together on the exercise that follows.

"Fair Fight" Rules

Fighting fairly requires that you and your partner share the same ground rules. Write as many rules as you can that you both can agree to, post them on the refrigerator, and use them to ground your disagreements.

Example: We will not fight in front of others (such as at a friend's dinner party).

Strategies for Effective Conflict

- Soften your startup—rather than blaming, begin gently by sharing how you feel.

- Say "I" rather than "You."

- Listen carefully and generously, acknowledging your partner's feelings and reflecting back what you understand from him or her.

- Address specific behaviour rather than personality traits or other generalities.

- When tension builds, monitor your own stress level and take a 20-minute or more break when necessary.

- Commit to being kind and respectful of your partner's differences and struggles.

- Learn to compromise and work toward a mutual "Yes."

Chapter 5

Vision

Oneness and "We-ness"

Christian union calls a couple not only to a lifetime of being for each other but also to a giving of self for the life of the world. The theme of *vision* invites you to consider your highest ideals and values for your partnership.

There are two sides to your vision: One is your vision for yourselves as individuals; the other is your vision and mission as a couple. Your ability to live out a call as a couple is connected to the peace you have made with your own unique call in the world. Discovering your call as a couple is a journey that twines in and out of your deepening sense of call as individuals.

Couples who enjoy a long life together have learned to protect each other's solitude (to paraphrase Rilke), to cherish that each has a unique call, a life that each is responsible to live well. But you also have a vocation as a couple in the world. Every couple bears witness to the astonishing power of love to endure, to rejoice, and to transform partners into more than each could have become alone.

Beyond that, you will want to pay attention to the values you hold together and the spirit of your partnership in the world. For example, if you value hospitality, how will your lives reflect that value? If you are called to be peacemakers in the world, how will you live out that call? If you place a high value on family, will you create family beyond your blood relations?

Some Questions to Explore as a Couple

Reflect on your vision as a couple:

1. What qualities/values do you believe contribute to a healthy relationship?
2. What do you enjoy doing together? apart?
3. Name three of your values. How are these expressed in your living? How might they be expressed in your marriage/covenant?
4. Name one of your partner's dreams. Can you share in it? Why or why not?

   Continue your story by working together on the exercise that follows.

Roots, Story, and Vision

Your Roots

What were your parents' or your family of origin's individual and shared values? If you grew up with two parents, what was their vision of their covenant/marriage? How do you hope to be like and unlike them?

Your Vision for Marriage/Covenant

Who is an inspiring couple for you? What do you sense about their values and their vision of their marriage/covenant? Take a few moments to jot down answers to these questions, then share your answers with your partner.

1. Some of the qualities I most admire in other couples' relationships are

   _____

   _____

   _____.

2. I would most like to have a relationship that resembles the relationship of

   _____

   _____

   _____.

3. I think the gifts you bring to our relationship that I most admire will be

   _____

   _____

   _____.

4. I think the gifts I will bring to our relationship will be

   _____

   _____

   _____.

Used with permission from *Getting Married: A Marriage Preparation Program,* © Humancare Associates, 905-841-3173.

Passion and Freedom

Chapter 6

Joy

Committing to Self-Giving

Seeking lifelong love and partnership commits a couple to joy in the deepest sense. *Joy* is not the absence of suffering. Indeed, many people have discovered that because they have experienced pain, they have opened themselves to love, compassion, and a deeper experience of joy. In the Christian context, a couple's relationship involves not only mutual care and erotic attraction between them but also the potential for a soul and flesh communion together that can reach out beyond themselves to intimacy with God.

When Jesus invites his friends to abide in his love, he further declares, "I have said these things to you so that my joy may be in you, and that your joy may be complete" (John 15:11). When you as a couple seek to grow in such long-term love and faithfulness, your relationship and commitment can become one of the primary places where this divine joy is experienced in the flesh.

The Risk of Intimacy

The United Church's *Gift, Dilemma and Promise* recognizes that

> all people experience a hunger for intimacy that is a profoundly spiritual matter, a hunger for God. It is in our experience of the intimate God that we find the grace and possibility of intimacy with one another.[1]

Although "intimacy" is sometimes a euphemism for sex, the two should not be confused. There can be deep, joyous intimacy between you as a couple outside and beyond your lovemaking. Weeping together, sharing laughter, even praying for and with each other may touch upon a profound intimacy. Likewise you may find your sexual passion bringing such joy that prayer or contemplative silence spontaneously erupts in the midst of your lovemaking to echo your pleasure. Many people have discovered that their most sacred moments have been in the arms of their beloved.

In marriage and any covenanted partnership, intimacy is like a dance, a movement of two people, coming together, drawing apart, moving in rhythm and counterpoint. That dance may pass through phases of shared struggle or suffering as well as joy, pain as well as happiness, sorrow as well as celebration. Especially close moments of the dance can be as simple as the embrace of shared silence that concludes a close conversation, or shared tears that may well up when both struggle to say sorry. It may come in the interweave of hands when walking with your beloved; the affectionate press of cheek, nose, and lip; or the more elaborate choreographies of flesh and spirit in the pleasures of lovemaking. This dance is a hunger for communion, a hunger for becoming one together in a mystery that plumbs the depths of body and spirit. As Jesus so simply and profoundly affirms for life partners, "So they are no longer two, but one flesh" (Mark 10:8b).

God's call to faithful long-term intimacy is a call to risk in self-giving. It can be a cause for deep peace and comfort, pleasure and happiness, even holy celebration. As you grow slowly into the fullness of your commitment, discovering yourself and each other—your similarities and differences, your blocks and weaknesses—intimacy can also be a cause for much pain and upheaval.

Your intention for lifelong union takes you on a path of discovering and bearing with each other's brokenness. It is also a commitment to being a companion to your beloved's deepest sufferings—for better or worse, in sickness and in health, in joy and in sorrow…. You may both long for and fear a lifetime of closeness and shared life. Life will offer unexpected joys, challenges, and suffering as you journey together. You commit yourselves to being companions through life right to the moment of death. There is always a cost, a surrender, and a mutual submission on the way to discovering the strength, joy, and love you make together as a couple.

Reflect on any couple you admire. How have these partners grown closer together, even through adversity? How do they touch your story? Share a specific time in which you and your partner have been challenged and yet have grown together in your relationship.

Some Questions to Explore as a Couple

Reflect on the spirit of joy in your relationship:

1. Describe an especially joyful time you have shared.

2. Recall a hard or difficult time in your life that helped you to grow into the person you are today—something you never would have chosen, but that has made you a more large-hearted human being. Can you share that experience with your partner?

3. Now remember a difficult or painful experience you have lived through together as a couple. Did you grow closer through it? Why or why not?

Continue your story by working together on the exercise that follows.

Note

1. *Gift, Dilemma and Promise: A Report and Affirmations on Human Sexuality* (Toronto: The United Church of Canada, 1984), p. 53. Used by permission.

Your Own Joy of Sex and Spirit

Twenty Statements for Your Pleasure

1. Things I especially enjoy doing with you: _____

   _____

2. Things I prefer to do alone: _____

   _____

3. What especially gives me joy and lifts my spirits: _____

   _____

4. I feel very close to you when _____

   _____

5. Expressions of affection I enjoy receiving: _____

   _____

   Expressions of affection I enjoy giving: _____

   _____

6. Touches that please me the most:_____

   _____

7. What I like best about my body: _____

   _____

8. Negative feelings I have about my body: _____

   _____

9. What I especially love about your body: _____

   _____

10. What I like about being a woman or a man: _____

    _____

    What I dislike: _____

    _____

11. How I learned about sex: _____

    _____

How this influenced my attitude and feelings about sex: _____

_____

12. What excites me sexually about you—what turns me on:

_____

_____

13. What I dislike or fear in our sexual relationship: _____

_____

14. I prefer physical affection in the
 ❏ morning ❏ afternoon ❏ night ❏ light ❏ dark

15. I feel free to express my sexual desires, preferences, likes, and dislikes to you.
 ❏ yes ❏ no

16. If I were to create an ideal atmosphere for our lovemaking, I would

_____

_____

17. When I'm feeling completely uninhibited I would like to _____

_____

_____

18. You would give me great pleasure if you would

_____

_____

19. With you, I have felt sexual or spiritual ecstasy, or a combined soaring of sex and spirit together. My description of this time:

_____

_____

20. With you, there are times of intimacy (sexual or other) when I have felt God especially close. My description of this time:

_____

_____

Part III

Middles:

Compassion and Renewal

Chapter 7

Marriage and Mid-Life Transitions

The Couple's Call

We've all come to know something new early in this 21st century: Our situation is precarious. We see this in our relationship to our environment, from the dramatic and unprecedented reduction in the water table to greenhouse gases to deforestation. We see it in our dependence on manufacturing weapons that get used in horrific wars that seem far away to Canadians.

In these times, a mature and joyful life partnership stands as a symbol. Our Roman Catholic sisters and brothers call it a sacrament: an outward and visible sign of God's invisible grace at work.

The curriculum of this school of committed lifelong partnership—forgiveness, faithfulness; brokenness, tenderness, vulnerability, shared laughter and tears, shared passion for each other and for all the earth—allows couples to be a light for others, a sign of love in the world. Christian couples work at finding a path of peace daily in their most intimate lives and, through that grace and discipline, are called by God to stand as peacemakers in our world. The fundamental call of couples is to establish a relationship that is loving and just, a relationship moving ever toward greater passion and freedom. We grow toward this call by choosing compassion and renewal.

Respecting Differences

It is in the daily round of living where compassion and renewal are needed: compassion to accept and even appreciate the things you cannot change, and renewal to rejoice in the things you can, to paraphrase the famous "Serenity Prayer" attributed to Reinhold Niebuhr:

> *God grant me the serenity*
> *to accept the things I cannot change*
> *courage to change the things I can*
> *and wisdom to know the difference.*

Together as a couple, you may want to consider these questions:

- What are the permanent differences in our relationship?

- How have we learned to negotiate the manifestations of those differences?

Chapter 8

Growing Together

Lifecycle Transitions

Below is a list of key transitional moments in many committed relationships. These stages are not prescriptive, but are meant only to help you understand more about possible issues that may arise. These are also good moments for you to pay attention to a need for extra time together; to pray together; to do a centring, renewing, or healing ritual; to take a special holiday; or to find some other significant way to mark the passage.

Common stages of a committed relationship include the following:

1. Early romantic enchantment.

2. Settling in and choosing more deeply: As couples live together, they deal in some way with the early tasks of negotiating power (see Chapter 4: Power).

3. If the partners become parents:

   - Children are born or welcomed.

   - Children start school.

   - Children grow into adolescents and then young adults.

   - Children leave home.

United Church Marriage Enrichment

Marriage Enrichment is a program that offers couples a weekend or several evenings away from home to focus on nurturing their relationship as a couple. Marriage Enrichment uses the dynamic process of group interaction: A variety of exercises encourages discussion between individual partners and with the group as a whole; lecture-type information-sharing is kept to a minimum.

Topics explored include couple communication, family of origin, dealing with differences, power and boundary issues, sexuality, and family rituals. These events are often held at one of the United Church education centres.

To find the nearest United Church education centre offering Marriage Enrichment, see www.united-church.ca/ministry/education/centres.shtm.

Source: Bob Jackson

---

4. Empty nest: The partners' needs here can differ or even reverse: A partner who has given primary attention to children may welcome a new career with creativity and energy, while a partner who has worked for decades may discover a new desire to slow down, spend more time on relationship rather than career, and nurture others more. In other words, partners can still surprise each other.

5. Retirement: In what's called the "new world of work," this transition can occur several times!

6. Growing old together: This is a time of setting priorities, facing illness, and needing new kinds of care and support.

7. Death of one partner: The surviving partner learns a new way of living (see Part IV).

Caring for aging parents often occurs somewhere in this cycle. For some couples, this is a distant responsibility; for others, it may include beginning a multi-generational household or mourning the loss of such a household.

Although each couple will face unique differences in the lifecycle of their lifelong partnership, every couple will live through some of these major transitions, as well as many other difficult and joyful times. For nearly half of Canadian couples, this lifecycle changes with separation and divorce. While the former partners will not be living through these transitions as a couple, many of these changes will proceed and continue to shape their relationships: their children's growth and needs, the death of the children's grandparents, and the eventual death of a former partner.

United Worldwide Marriage Encounter

United Worldwide Marriage Encounter offers couples a weekend away from home to enable them to gain a deeper and richer relationship through a better understanding of self and spouse. As well, Marriage Encounter is an opportunity for couples to deepen their relationship with God.

The program consists of a series of presentations in which the leaders (couples and clergy from the United Church) share their own experiences on a variety of subjects. Each presentation is followed by an opportunity for participants to reflect privately on a related question. Couples are then given time alone to explore their thoughts and feelings with each other (it is a very private event; there is no group discussion). Participants are taught techniques to help make this experience a positive and nurturing one.

For more information, see www.uwwme.org or call 1-800-795-LOVE.

Couples and Mid-Life

I have been completely surprised and delighted by the sparkle within my own mid-life marriage. Conventional wisdom would suggest that marital bliss is at its height for newlyweds—they have, for example, the best sex—and you can expect things to go downhill from there.

And things will go downhill when we don't make a conscious decision to do something different. But I beg to differ with conventional wisdom. It seems to me that our middle years of marriage have so far been our best, largely because we've decided to invest in our relationship. We now take time for one another in the midst of mature responsibilities, with annual, monthly, weekly, and daily rituals and commitments that we didn't make earlier on. I suppose it's because we were taking our love for granted back then. But now, we see it as too precious to take for granted. It's grown in value. And we also notice the withering ravages of time in relationships where love has been neglected. We don't want that to happen to us.

* * *

But what happens when we look at that well-worn, aging face and form, that person who is not the same one we married because there have been so many changes, and we have to decide whether or not we'll say "yes" to a renewed life with this person or "no, it's just not worth it"?

Saying "yes" to the possibility of renewing love is, I believe, a divine act. I see in Jesus a person who said "yes" to God, to a spirit-led life of disciplined love. And one of the ways in which you could tell that he said "yes" to God was in the way he loved, regardless of people's limitations and foibles.

Fidelity to God requires that kind of openness to the spiritual themes and variations that erupt at every stage of our lives. We need to take our challenges for personal growth seriously. And what a blessing when we are able to explore those themes—the ones that are deeply personal and the others that have grown out of years of loving relationship—by saying "yes" to our beloved: Yes, this relationship is worth renewing over and over again. Yes, I intend to be with you to the end of life.

Then God really surprises us with a love that's better than ever.

Source: Mardi Tindal

Qualities of a Lasting Marriage

What do lasting marriages have in common? A study carried out in Toronto included interviews with 129 couples who had been married for an average of 25 years. The study identified 10 items most of the couples found important:[1]

- *respect for each other*
- *trusting each other*
- *loyalty*
- *loving each other*
- *counting on each other*
- *considering each other's needs*
- *providing each other with emotional support*
- *commitment to make the marriage last*
- *fidelity*
- *and a give and take in marriage*

Also important: "a sense of humour, friendship, companionship, honesty, caring for each other, commitment to the marriage, and a good sexual life."[2]

Gay Life Partners

As a gay couple, we have never lacked for challenges in our individual and collective lives over the 26 years that we have been together. Within a few months of when we met, fell in love, and started living together in 1976, my partner's employer launched action to fire him because he was gay and he was also diagnosed with multiple sclerosis. In the early 1990s, I tested positive for HIV.

Sharing a deep spirituality and Christian faith has been critical not only to our survival together but indeed has also allowed us to thrive. My partner's early background was as a very committed Catholic. He harbours deep resentment toward that Church because of its rejection of gays generally and him specifically. I am from a United Church background and I am grateful for the support that I have experienced as an openly gay person in this church. The faith and values that my partner and I share transcend the varying experiences that we have had with institutional churches. We know that we are loved by God.

We do not shy away from witnessing to our faith among friends, both gay and straight, in this increasingly secularized world. Opportunities regularly present themselves in which we are able sometimes in quiet, simple ways and sometimes more explicitly to share our gratitude to God for the gifts of love and creation and to express our commitment to justice as followers of Jesus. Though the future is unpredictable and sure to be filled with further challenges, we look forward to sharing our lives together and supporting each other till death do us part.

Source: David Hallman

Some Questions to Explore as a Couple

Think about your relationship and answer these questions:

1. What qualities of your relationship have sustained you?
2. What are you missing?
3. What do you need now?

    Continue your story by working together on the exercises that follow.

Notes

1. Benjamin Schlesinger, "Lasting Marriages in the 1980s," *Conciliation Courts Review,* 20 (1982): 42–49. Quoted in Benjamin Schlesinger, "Strengths in Families: Accentuating the Positive," The Vanier Institute of the Family, *Contemporary Family Trends Series* (1998). Retrieved June 2003 from www.vifamily.ca/cf/pubs/strength.htm. Used by permission of The Vanier Institute of the Family.
2. Ibid.

Mid-Life Change and Growth Checklist

In what areas of your relationship would you like to change and grow in new ways? In the following checklist, put a check mark beside your areas of concern using a scale of 0 to 5.

Share your checklist with your partner. Are there areas you would like to work on together, or areas you might need help addressing?

Statement	0 not an issue	1	2	3	4	5 major concern
I would like to have more quality time with you.	___	___	___	___	___	___
I would like us each to have more independence.	___	___	___	___	___	___
I wish we could communicate better with each other.	___	___	___	___	___	___
I wish we paid more attention to the spiritual side of our relationship.	___	___	___	___	___	___
I would like our sex life to be more satisfying.	___	___	___	___	___	___
I wish we had more romance in our relationship.	___	___	___	___	___	___
I want more fun in our life together.	___	___	___	___	___	___
I want us to more actively work for peace.	___	___	___	___	___	___
I want to discuss how we can take care of the environment.	___	___	___	___	___	___
I would like it if we were more organized.	___	___	___	___	___	___
I wish we would share the household chores more fairly.	___	___	___	___	___	___
I wish we could manage our finances better.	___	___	___	___	___	___

Mid-Life Change and Growth Checklist (Continued)

Statement	0 not an issue	1	2	3	4	5 major concern
I would like you to share more of the work.	___	___	___	___	___	___
I would like my relationship with our children to improve.	___	___	___	___	___	___
I would like your relationship with our children to improve.	___	___	___	___	___	___
I want to improve my relationship with our families.	___	___	___	___	___	___
I wish your relationship with our families would improve.	___	___	___	___	___	___
I wish we had fewer differences in basic values and goals in life.	___	___	___	___	___	___
I wish we could agree more about friends.	___	___	___	___	___	___
I wish there was less fighting between us.	___	___	___	___	___	___
I wish we could learn to fight more openly or constructively.	___	___	___	___	___	___
I would like to feel more respected in our relationship.	___	___	___	___	___	___
I would like to feel more free in our relationship.	___	___	___	___	___	___
I would like to feel less lonely in our relationship.	___	___	___	___	___	___
I wish we could do some new things together.	___	___	___	___	___	___
I wish we had more purpose in our life together.	___	___	___	___	___	___
I want us to give more to our world.	___	___	___	___	___	___

A Gift of Memory

Take as much time as you need to write your thoughts in the spaces provided, and then share your responses with your partner.

1. When we were first a couple, we wanted to change or at least affect the world by

   _____

   _____.

2. Our biggest dreams were

   _____

   _____.

3. I/you/we have done that by

   _____

   _____.

4. We have discovered these other dreams, desires, and priorities in our life together:

   _____

   _____

   _____.

5. How I feel about these evolving priorities:

   _____

   _____

   _____.

6. The way we have experienced God's presence and call in our lives together is

   _____

   _____

   _____.

A Gift of Imagination

1. How many more years we expect to have together, if all goes well:

    _____

    _____

2. Our greatest gifts as a couple:

    _____

    _____

    _____

3. The unique gifts we offer to others:

    _____

    _____

    _____

4. What we still want to do in the world:

    _____

    _____

    _____

5. Our biggest dreams now:

    _____

    _____

    _____

    _____

6. Practical steps we could take to continue to be the kind of people
    we dream of being:

    _____

    _____

    _____

    _____

Your Intimacy Intelligence

Circle "Yes" or "No" for statements 1–10:

1.	I'm aware of your hopes and dreams.	Yes	No
2.	You are familiar with my aspirations.	Yes	No
3.	I periodically ask you how you are feeling.	Yes	No
4.	I know your major current concerns.	Yes	No
5.	You are familiar with my current stresses.	Yes	No
6.	I can tell others about your key beliefs about life.	Yes	No
7.	I feel that you know me well.	Yes	No
8.	You know who my good friends are.	Yes	No
9.	I am familiar with what you do at work.	Yes	No
10.	I know what especially delights you.	Yes	No

11. Three of your most important values:

_____

_____

_____

12. Some things that really please you:

_____

_____

13. Some of your current major worries:

_____

_____

14. Some of your favourite music:

_____

_____

Your Intimacy Intelligence (Continued)

15. Some of your most important friends:

_____

_____

_____

16. Three especially significant times in your life:

_____

_____

_____

17. Some of your major aspirations in life:

_____

_____

_____

18. Three significant things that happened to you as a child:

_____

_____

_____

19. Some of your special interests:

_____

_____

_____

20. Some things you would want to do if we had the resources:

_____

_____

_____

A Date with Your Mate

Have a fun date with your partner: Go on a picnic, wear unusual clothes, make love somewhere different, eat fabulous foods, go to an art gallery or museum, take a long walk in nature, or explore a nearby town, backroad, or part of a city you haven't been to. Use your imagination!

Say you've gone out together, you're having a great time, and you want to have meaningful, soul-connecting, intimacy-building conversation, but you can't think of anything significant or interesting to talk about. Try some of these as appetizers:

- Who influenced you when you were growing up?

- Whom did you admire?

- Some people believe we know the most about our unique purpose in the world, our life work, before adolescence. What did you love to do before you were 10—what could absorb your whole interest and attention? Does that have any relation to how you spend your time now?

- What was your most significant spiritual experience?

- How do you want to be remembered after you die?

- What song lyrics do you remember from your teen years? Why do you think they've stayed in your head?

- What were your favourite toys or books when you were growing up?

- What is the first joke you can remember?

- What are your three favourite movies of all time or the first that comes to mind? What does that say about you?

Compassion and Forgiveness

This is an exercise for a time of struggle and pain between you, adapted from a simple, beautiful exercise from the Buddhist tradition.

1. Find a place where you and your partner can have at least 10 uninterrupted minutes to yourself.

2. Let yourself feel the feelings that are upsetting you or are a result of conflict as fully and completely as possible.

3. Accept these feelings without judgment: They are what make you human and, like the weather, just are. Even greet them affectionately by name: "Hello my anger!" "Dear little insecurities, I see you are back today," "Oh, fear, you've grown!" Part of growing in passion and freedom is feeling your feelings fully, then allowing that experience to help you grow.

4. Now breathe in deeply and become aware that millions and millions of people in the world are feeling those same feelings right now! Become conscious that you belong to this huge human family.

5. Send your compassion out to all those people. You know just how they feel, and you feel with them. Somewhere in the world, people you will never know are likewise sending their compassion to you.

6. After 10 or 15 minutes, begin or have your partner begin to hum gently a song for all the people in the world. Try "Kum Ba Yah" or a song you know your partner especially likes. The other partner should join in when she or he is ready.

7. Look into each other's eyes, and offer each other a few words of understanding and appreciation. This doesn't mean your difference or hurt is resolved: There may be the hard work of communication and negotiation ahead. What you have done right now is to put your struggle into a larger context and chosen compassion toward each other.

Lovers' Workout to Build Healthy Relational Muscles

This is an easy workout to help you tone up and feel better. You might try inventing and going into training for your own Extreme Lovers' Workout!

- *Morning:* Take three minutes each to learn one thing that is happening in your beloved's life each day.

- *Later:* Be sure to greet your partner with affection for at least two minutes when you see each other again after being apart.

- *Daily check-in:* Take 20 minutes for a conversation at the end of the workday to debrief and share about the day. Keep caught up on each other's plans, hopes, desires, and so on. At the end of this time, see if you each can name three things you appreciate and want to encourage in each other.

- Hug your partner at least twice a day!

- Kiss, hold, touch, and cuddle each other every day.

- Make sure to embrace each other before going to sleep. If you can, in that tender closeness let go of any minor irritations or resentments that have built up over the day.

- *Weekly date:* Set aside an hour or two or three once a week for being with your beloved exclusively. Do something fun, romantic, or special to reconnect and cherish each other. Enjoy!

Retreat to Deepen Love and Connection

Jesus said, "For where two or three are gathered in my name, I am there among them" (Matthew 18:20). The smallest unit of church, then, is two. This retreat assumes the two of you are "church" and invites you to hear the United Church Creed as your own.

This retreat can be two sessions on a reserved day or two evenings of a weekend, or perhaps you could look ahead and reserve two separate weeks when you can find extra time at lunch and during the evening to spend together. Just jump in and enjoy this retreat with your partner.

Remember: This is supposed to be fun and something you wish to commit yourselves to. If it is important enough, you'll find the time!

Session 1: Learning to Trust

Gospel
Jesus at the wedding at Cana (John 2:1–11)

Ritual
Choose one or more rituals that feel right for you:

- Bring a drink to share with your partner, maybe one that in some way recalls the mystery of your initial attraction to your partner.

- Remember and tell (again!) the story of your early attraction to your partner, and then the story of your growing desire for your partner.

- Make a card recalling and celebrating your beginnings in love. Or perhaps begin a small book of your story together.

Blessing
Light a candle, hold hands, and simply sit together in silence, aware of God creating you and changing you from water into wine, from your beginnings into something more full-bodied and tasty! Finish by saying together the first half of the United Church Creed:

> We are not alone,
> > we live in God's world.
>
> We believe in God:
> > who has created and is creating,
> > who has come in Jesus,
> > > the Word made flesh,
> > > to reconcile and make new,
> > who works in us and others
> > > by the Spirit.

Passion and Freedom

Session 2: Called to Hunger and Work Together

Gospel
Jesus feeds the multitude (Mark 6:35–44)

Ritual
Choose one or more rituals that feel right for you:
- Contribute toward a late-night meal for your beloved. Make the table beautiful and the setting special with flowers, beautiful napkins, and so on.

- Talk about what you especially enjoy doing together. Remember a time of working or serving together, doing something for creation or for other people.

- What is the call of your relationship? What is your dream, plan, or hope together to serve each other and to serve God's world?

- Start a storybook about the two of you. Together, write about a desire, dream, or plan you have for the coming year and for the coming decade.

Say together:

> We trust in God.
>
> We are called to be the Church:
> > to celebrate God's presence,
> > to live with respect in Creation,
> > to love and serve others,
> > to seek justice and resist evil,
> > to proclaim Jesus, crucified and risen,
> > > our judge and our hope.
> In life, in death, in life beyond death,
> > God is with us.
> We are not alone.
>
> > Thanks be to God.

Blessing
Tenderly feed each other the final part of your meal. Spend the rest of the evening holding each other with respect and tenderness. Fall asleep together.

Your Vows

Your vows are the most public, intimate, and sacred promises you will ever make. It is good to often recall together what you have promised!

A married minister wrote that this exercise is a good one because at times the reality of the promises is all that holds us together. The commitment implicit in the promise made is important.

Take time to remember what you promised. What do you think of as you read your vows? What images from your life together come to mind? Jot down some of those memories or images beside each phrase.

_____

_____

_____

_____

_____

_____

_____

_____

_____

_____

_____

_____

_____

_____

_____

_____

_____

_____

_____

_____

Life Integration

Books about aging tell us that the psychological task of our older years is life integration. This must be done individually, as we come to terms with our life. Integration is also a task of couples. Here are three exercises on life integration.

Living and Dying Well

> Are we preparing ourselves for our death, or are we ignoring death by keeping busy? Are we helping each other to die, or do we simply assume we are going to always be here for each other? Will our death give new life, new hope, and new faith to our friends, or will it be no more than another cause for sadness? The main question is not, How much will we still be able to do during the few years we have left to live? but rather, How can we prepare ourselves for our death in such a way that our dying will be a new way for us to send our and God's Spirit to those whom we have loved and who have loved us?
>
> OUR GREATEST GIFT by HENRI J.M. NOUWEN. Copyright © 1994 by Henri J.M. Nouwen. Reprinted by permission of HarperCollins Publishers Inc.

Write a letter to your partner saying what thoughts, feelings, and hopes are sparked by reading the above reflection.

See also Stephen Levine, *A Year to Live: How to Live This Year as if It Were Your Last*, rev. ed. (New York: Bell Tower, 1998).

A Life Storybook

You can work on this for yourself or create it as a surprise for your partner or as an anniversary memento. Ask friends and family to write a note, either on the spot at a party or mailed later to you, about you or the two of you as a couple. What memories stand out? What have you or you and your partner together contributed to their lives? If there has been pain, how has it been resolved? Assemble all the letters, notes, and photos into a beautiful scrapbook.

A book like this can become a heritage. It is truthful, affirming, and often very moving. It can introduce people to you as an individual or a couple. You may also choose to include your own pictures or thoughts on your growth as individuals and as a couple.

Ethical Wills

An ethical will is a Jewish tradition that you can complete as a couple. Write a simple document summing up what you have learned in your lives together. What is the wisdom, the spirit you most wish to pass on? What do you hope for your loved ones? Give this ethical will to your loved ones now, or place it with your other wills.

For more information on ethical wills, see Jack Riemer and Nathaniel Stampfer, eds., *So That Your Values Live On: Ethical Wills and How to Prepare Them* (Woodstock, VT: Jewish Lights, 1994).

Chapter 9

Growing Apart

Introduction

Every relationship has highs and lows. However, if the lows predominate, a couple will likely grow apart and find other people, places, and things to sustain them as individuals. One or both partners may seek out a minister at such times. Many issues contribute to the lows in any relationship. What follows is a discussion of only a few of these issues.

Some Questions to Explore as a Couple

Reflect on some or all of the following questions:

1. What issues do you think need to be addressed?

2. What would help you address these issues?

3. What areas do you need to work on alone? as a couple?

4. Do you need professional help—such as sexual abuse counselling, drug addiction counselling, psychiatric help—to address your issues?

5. If other family members are involved, such as children, how are you helping them cope with this struggle in your relationship?

6. Despite the pain in your relationship right now, as you seek to walk through it, is there anything you can celebrate or hold onto that can help you get through this time?

7. How might the church help you?

Affairs

Statistics suggest that affairs (defined most simply as one person secretly having sex with someone other than the person's partner) affect anywhere from 30 to 60 percent of marriages or long-term partnerships. Interestingly, most marriages survive an affair. In fact, some recent research suggests that up to 80 percent of those who divorce during an affair ultimately regret their decision.[1]

As with most of life's deepest pain and confusion, there are no right answers to questions such as "Should I tell my partner that I had an affair even though it's over?" Experts offer every conceivable answer, but people have to choose what feels right to them.

Affairs have particular emotional complexity. The betrayed partner can feel angry, rejected, and filled with a deep sense of loss, grief, and fear. The partner having the affair may be feeling attractive and valuable, or deeply ashamed and humiliated.

This we know to be true: No matter how much of a mess we've created, God loves us and is on our side. God offers us new beginnings, wanting us to use even the most shattering experiences of our lives to grow, to become bigger people, to deepen our compassion, and to live more fully in truth and love. And working through these times of emergency—crisis moments when we are emerging into a new phase—takes time. Betrayal may lead to new growth, but first it must be lived through in all its full range of pain, anger, and fear.

If you are in this situation, seek out someone—your minister, a counsellor, a trusted friend—to be with you in your pain and confusion, someone who will listen to you with compassion and encourage you to be honest.

Physical Change and Aging Bodies

Healthy intimacy is often related to how "at home" a person feels in his or her body. Our bodies are both a gift and a responsibility to care for. Our society tends to be unmerciful about aging bodies, and yet the reality is that all bodies age. With the aging process come changes that can affect how people feel about their body and what their body is capable of.

The Christian faith honours that we are incarnate people; until our death, we are inseparable from our bodies. Lovers have the most profound physical and spiritual union.

Recognizing Physical Issues

At times, physical issues can manifest themselves as spiritual issues or psychological problems. Various medications can affect a person's sexual function, mood, ability to handle anger, energy level, and impulse control. They can also produce headaches, fatigue, and a number of other changes that influence couples' lives. It can be helpful to ask your physician or pharmacist to answer questions about the side-effects of any new medication you are taking.

Sex for Seniors

I have a cranky, young doctor who insists on outrageous prescriptions for what ails me. Like exercise. I prefer to get my exercise jumping to conclusions. He wants me to spend half an hour a day on that mind-numbing devil's invention, the stationary bike. Then he adds cheerfully, "Sex is good exercise too!" This, after he's just written a prescription for a medication that effectively takes the stuffing out of the old sock.

My late friend, Bob Hatfield, a medical doctor, often prescribed laughter as a good exercise. And it's true. A good belly-laugh is "internal jogging" and releases as many endorphins into the brain as a handful of aspirin. And a good belly-laugh does much the same sort of thing, physiologically, as an orgasm. Which is great news at my age, because you can do it with anyone, anytime. And you can manage it more than once a month.

* * *

Big news for everyone under 60! Coital sex is not the main show! It's nice when it happens, but it's way down on the priority list from things like intimacy, tenderness, closeness. Reclaiming your virginity, I sometimes call it.

Shakespeare almost had it almost right. He talked about "second childishness." That happens for some and it's sad. But what's really great is "second childlikeness." A small child knows it needs tenderness and closeness. For me, one of the delights of grandparenting is to have Jake or Zoë come and climb on my lap. It doesn't occur to them to ask permission. They know they are welcome. They also know they need that closeness and that tenderness. In a healthy family it is always there for them. But believe me, grandpa and grandma need it as much as they do. Just as I need those many moments of closeness with Bev throughout the day and at night in bed.

Of course that's a form of sexuality. Or sensuality. Call it what you like. It's been said that men give tenderness in order to get sex, and women give sex in order to get tenderness. I have no idea whether that is true or not, but in healthy senior relationships, we give tenderness in order to get tenderness. Coital sex happens sometimes, of course. And that's nice. But the tenderness, the intimacy, is just as fulfilling when it doesn't.

This concept is very important for those of us who are in a good, happy, long-term relationship. But it is even more important for those who aren't, but would like to be.

Source: Both excerpts by Ralph Milton, "Sex for Seniors," from *The Practice of Ministry in Canada*. Used by permission. Ralph Milton edits a free on-line newsletter called *Rumors* for active Christians with a sense of humour. See www.joinhands.com.

Sexual Abuse

The official policy statement on sexual abuse of The United Church of Canada says:

> Sexual abuse shall refer to demeaning/exploitative behaviour of a sexual nature ranging from jokes, to unwanted touching, to forced sexual activities. It may also include threats of such behaviour. Abusive sexual acts are primarily acts of power. Sexual harassment, sexual assault and pastoral sexual misconduct are forms of sexual abuse.[2]

Sexual abuse, which often occurs over a long period of time, has an impact on the victim's life and relationships. The abuse itself is a traumatic experience that leaves emotional and physical scars. Disclosing the abuse is a painful and difficult process for victims. Unfortunately, at times the victim's story is not believed, people react with panic or horror, or the victim is treated as "bad" and is shunned by others. Survivors of sexual abuse speak of the pain that is intensified by isolation, and how that pain eases when it is shared.

Healing can occur when victims' silence is broken and their pain confronted. But healing occurs at each individual's own pace, through hard work and trusting, caring, and committed relationships with others. Everyone deserves to be treated with dignity and respect at all times, but this is especially true during the healing process.

Many people will need therapy to walk through the pain of sexual abuse. This might involve both partners as you seek to find wholeness and health in your relationship.

Notes

1. John Gottman with Nan Silver, *Why Marriages Succeed or Fail: And How You Can Make Yours Last* (New York: Fireside, 1995).
2. The United Church of Canada, *Sexual Abuse (Sexual Harassment, Pastoral Sexual Misconduct, Sexual Assault) and Child Abuse: Official Policy and Procedures Document* (Toronto: The United Church of Canada, revised April 2000), p. 4. Used by permission.

Part IV

Endings:

Grief, Mystery, and New Beginnings

Chapter 10

The Grief Journey

Grief and Forgiveness

The daily physical life together of every couple in life partnership has an endpoint. Lumping together death, separation, abandonment, and divorce or covenant ending as this section does is awkward, since each of these experiences is very different. Still, grief can be experienced during or after any loss. The spiritual journey of grief is our most profound and difficult journey into becoming more deeply part of the human race.

Stages of Grief

Despite the current trend of describing and delineating the "grief process," the actual stages of grief are not linear, predictable, or absolute. There are as many ways of grieving as there are human beings. The point of setting out some experiences that seem to be shared by many people is not to make these experiences or emotions prescriptive, but rather to increase our awareness of them and to reassure us.

In her ground-breaking book *On Death and Dying*,[1] Elisabeth Kübler-Ross observed five emotional states that people facing their own deaths progressed through:

1. denial

2. anger

3. bargaining

4. depression

5. acceptance

What Kübler-Ross's work did was to acknowledge these extreme emotions as normal, and demonstrate that each was valid and even necessary—not a state to be rescued from, but part of a sacred passage. The five stages were soon recognized as helpful for dealing with many kinds of grieving. Sometimes three stages are more useful than five: denial; then a middle stage in which a person circles around and back through anger, bargaining, and depression; and eventually some form of acceptance. People can revisit these stages repeatedly. Our emotional growth is like an onion skin or spiral: We revisit our key moments of pain and growth over and over, deepening our integration of those experiences into our lives.

Here is another way to frame stages of grief, adapted from *Surviving Grief...and Learning to Live Again* by Catherine M. Sanders:[2]

1. *Shock:* This is a period of alarm, disbelief, confusion, and unreality.

2. *Awareness of loss:* This is a time of intense stress, separation anxiety, yearning, frustration, anger, guilt, and sleep disturbance. It can be marked by conflict, contradictory emotional expectations, and vivid dreams. A support group can be especially helpful through this stage.

3. *Conservation and the need to withdraw:* This stage can begin months or up to a year after the loss. It may come at a time of diminished social support, when it seems like the loss is in the past. The stage can look like depression or even despair. People in this stage feel like pulling back into themselves. They may feel helpless, out of control, sickly, weak, and exhausted; may need more sleep; and may find themselves reviewing the loss obsessively. This can go on for many months or years, and reviewing the loss can take people back to relive previous stages. Gradually, for most people, there comes a turning point.

4. *Turning point:* This may be three or more years later. At this point the person begins to resume control of his or her life. This may involve relinquishing the role that was lost after the death or divorce or covenant ending, or even giving up the role of mourner. People in this stage are able to form a new identity, centring themselves. They begin to forgive the pain and to take care of themselves and their own needs. Horizons seem to expand, and people may search for the larger human meaning of their experience. This can also mark a turning point of being able to reach out to others again.

What is especially important here is the long time this journey can take. Some people have begun their grieving long before the loss, and by the time the separation comes they have already accepted it on some level. But no one can live an experience fully until she or he is in it, and after the initial relief of getting through the loss, people can be quite unsettled by renewed cycling through the grief process.

Stages of Forgiveness

Forgiveness is often a related part of the grief journey, though less has been written about it. In her excellent article "Ripped Apart," Molly Layton suggests "forgiveness often proceeds along a path from stunned innocence to the tortures of obsession to a surprising expansion of meaning."[3] These three stages—innocence, obsession, and transcendence—each force the person who feels wronged to revise assumptions about the world and self. The ultimate direction, Layton compellingly argues, is expansion of ourselves as people, and in how we function in the world.

In *Becoming Human*, Jean Vanier sets out a series of choices that move toward forgiveness and reconciliation. He too believes "At the heart of forgiveness is the desire to be liberated from negative passions, from sharp dislikes and hatred."[4] Vanier suggests that three basic principles underlie forgiveness of others and of ourselves: believing that we are all part of a common humanity, believing that each of us can evolve and change, and yearning for unity and peace, for true liberation.

David Augsburger, a Mennonite pastor and psychotherapist, states that forgiveness is the restoration of right relationships between two people.[5] Forgiveness is a process, not a single act. When two people desire to move toward right relationship by recognizing wrong and hurt and letting go of unjust demands, the process of forgiveness can begin. For Augsburger, forgiveness needs to go two ways: Hurt needs to be recognized, and genuine repentance needs to be offered. Augsburger contends that when these elements are not present, a person needs to care enough not to forgive. He does not suggest that a person remain forever in a state of not forgiving the other person; instead, the hurt person should keep heart and mind open to the possibility of forgiveness and to do the work that is possible within her or his own soul to come to terms with and let go of the control the hurt has on her or his life. Sometimes this involves forgiving oneself.

Being Single Again

Being single again is a new reality if you have lost a life partner, a reality that can result in an identity crisis. However, singlehood can be an opportunity to reflect on life as it has been, to question daily routines, and to set new priorities. Losing a loved one requires people to discover parts of themselves that may not have been developed or needed before. It requires that a person see him- or herself through an entirely different lens of singleness, a time of knowing oneself in a new way. In *Living Your Dying*, Stanley Keleman writes, "Endings bring us face to face with the unknown. Endings force us to make new relationships, or at least offer that opportunity…. Many people will say 'that person is irreplaceable to me.' The truth of the matter is that making an ending forces us to start being more self-reliant, or at least offers that opportunity."[6]

Some singles find support and comfort in their faith community. At its best, the church is a place to help all who come through its doors to know or reaffirm that they are wondrous, unique creations of God who are deeply loved and called to abundant life to live fully their life's passion and freedom. Most of all, we need to be open to God's help to strengthen relationships—to restore love, to enable forgiveness, and to renew covenant.

Being single can also change a person's financial reality, which can limit life's choices in significant ways. It is helpful to seek financial advice if you are in this situation. Bank managers are good sources who do not charge for their time.

When a Loved One Has Died

It matters how a person died; every loss is different and every death is different. The surviving partner may need to talk about the death and tell how it happened over and over. As well, some survivors feel guilty. Linda Feinberg's book *I'm Grieving as Fast as I Can* is a useful resource for understanding how different people cope with grief.[7]

You may need to be especially attentive if one of the following scenarios is your reality:

- If you are a young widow/widower, the loss of your partner may frighten your friends and isolate you as the grieving partner.

- If your partner committed suicide, your grief may be further complicated by horror, anger, and shame.

- If you weren't publicly married, you may be an unacknowledged mourner. This is an especially painful danger for gay, lesbian, and bisexual partners whose relationship was not "out" or whose union was not recognized by their families.

- The tragic, sudden death or murder of a partner may elicit strong waves of anger, bitterness, and hatred. Find out whether a support group is available for survivors, or try to find others who have suffered similar experiences.

- If you broke up with your partner before he or she died, know that no matter how civil or bitter a breakup has been, and no matter how long ago it occurred, the death of a former life partner can bring grief to the survivor. It is reasonable and legitimate for you to grieve. If you cannot go to the funeral, visitation, or memorial, create a ritual or liturgy to mark the end of your former partner's life, if possible. Your minister may be able to help you with this.

It is important, as you are able, to feel the full range of emotions of grief, not repressing or denying how terrible your loss is. Take care of yourself now, and also listen to your heart. Sometimes people who are grieving discover a new call arising from their loss, their pain leading them to work for others or for a better world.

When You Are Divorcing or Ending Your Covenant

Ending a life partnership through divorce or covenant ending may be the best choice in a devastating set of options, but the failure of a committed relationship can be a crushing experience.

The United Church chooses to stand in solidarity with the crushed and broken-hearted. We want to help those living this terrible passage to land on their feet, to know that God still loves them tenderly and calls them even to use this pain of failure to be God's presence in the world.

Times of transition and chaos can also be times of creativity and growth. Even betrayal forces people to recreate their lives if they can find in themselves the inner courage to fully engage their experience. In her book *The Good Divorce*, Constance Ahrons notes that people going through a divorce list a variety of feelings, not all of them negative: They may feel pain, loneliness, anger, stress, grief, stigma, and failure, *and* freedom, relief, strength, hope, courage, happiness, and dignity.[8]

Some people find that it helps to keep long-term goals in mind, such as keeping their family together, supporting their children through the process,

---

Sex and the Single Senior

As the population ages, there are more and more single seniors. Most of them are women. In conversations with some of them, I learned that they long—they ache sometimes—for intimacy. They yearn for a familiar voice to greet them in the morning, and someone to offer a long hug when life feels uncertain.

There are not enough men to go around. And of the men there are, too many are spooked by the unreal expectations around sex that are implicit in so much that hammers us from the media. All the media coverage of Viagra has made the problem worse, because we hear the implication behind all the hoopla. If you can't get it up, you're only half a man. We men grew up with this load of expectations around sex, and we need help to set it down so we can enter a relationship based on tenderness and companionship and intimacy. The testosterone tango is killing us.

The homophobic bugaboo is involved there too. Of course, many women prefer to live by themselves, but for those that don't, wouldn't it be great if they felt free to enter into a relationship with another woman that would help them fill their childlike need for warmth and friendship?

Here's my plea to my many friends in pastoral work. Help us understand our sexuality. Find ways to say to those of us who are seniors, that age is not a disease but is, as Paul Tournier once said, "The Sabbath of our lives." It is a time when we can focus on our primary values, our essential needs. A time when we can rediscover our childhood, when the thing we wanted most was to be loved, cared for, supported, laughed with, affirmed. Someone to share the last, and sometimes very frightening lap, of our human journey.

Source: Ralph Milton, "Sex for Seniors," from *The Practice of Ministry in Canada*. Used by permission. Ralph Milton edits a free on-line newsletter called *Rumors* for active Christians with a sense of humour. See www.joinhands.com.

---

integrating the divorce into their life, even choosing who they want to be. If the relationship has been abusive, the primary concern is the safety of the non-abusive partner and any children.

Even decades after the end of a life partnership, for the sake of something bigger than themselves—the birth of a grandchild or a major illness of their child, for example—estranged and bitter couples can find peace with each other and their history. It is never too late for healing to happen.

Rituals

These rituals are simply some ways to sit with your own heart and with your own journey as you face the loss that touches and changes your life.

Brain-Drain Pages

Write daily "brain-drain" pages in a notebook or journal. Morning is the best time to do this. As soon as you wake up, start to write as fast as you can, without editing, anything that comes to mind. Pour everything out on the page. Keep your hand moving for at least three pages, even if what you are writing seems like junk or gibberish. The writing is for no one's eyes but your own, and even you should not read these pages for at least several months. Although this may not seem like a very significant exercise, this fast, unedited writing can help you name your experience and make some sense of your loss.

Sacred Loss Space

Set up a private place in your home to place symbols of your loss and your inner state—symbols of grief, loss, forgiveness, anger, memories, and so on. These can change and evolve over days and weeks. You might place a candle among these symbols and just sit quietly with them, perhaps praying, just breathing, and simply letting God's Spirit be in all that is there.

Ethical Will

Ethical wills are a Jewish tradition in which a person writes a simple document summing up what he or she has learned in life. You may wish to record what you learned in the life with your former partner. What is the wisdom, the spirit, you most wish to pass on? What do you hope for your loved ones? If your partner has died, you can also record her or his legacy, give it to your loved ones, or place it with your will.

For more on ethical wills, see *So That Your Values Live On: Ethical Wills and How to Prepare Them*.[9]

Mandala

Artwork can be a gentle and powerful way to draw people into the present. A mandala is a circular piece of art that radiates out of the centre. Creating one is a simple, focused exercise. While it is the process, not the product, that is important, mandalas are satisfying because they generally evolve into something beautiful!

Take a large sheet of white paper and watercolour paints, pastels, crayons, or other medium. Put on relaxing music. Begin by drawing a small circle in the centre of the paper. Then draw or paint a full ring of pattern around the central circle. Add more rings of pattern one by one, like the rings in a tree trunk that tell its age. There is no theme or purpose: Just do what feels good.

Letting Go

On a sheet of paper, write your initial dreams for your relationship. Put a check mark beside or write about the ones that were realized. Acknowledge those that can never be fulfilled in the context of the relationship. Are there other ways to fulfill these hopes now? In the context of prayer and scripture (some selections follow below), burn the sheet of paper, reclaiming its energy for transformation and asking God's Spirit to bathe you with healing and blessing as you let go.

End of Marriage/Covenant Liturgy

A parting ceremony can be an important step in the process of divorce or covenant ending. The ceremony calls forth the healing power of gathering in community and gives your family and friends permission to grieve together. It also names a moment of closure and defines the liturgical beginning of new, separate lives. Such a ceremony helps you and your former partner name your loss and any sense of failure, and commit yourselves to whatever healing and goodwill is possible. Inviting friends into relationship with each of you also helps friends know what is expected of them now.

You might ask your minister to perform the "Service Marking the End of a Covenant" from *Celebrate God's Presence*, pages 710–15.[10] The benediction at the end of the service (page 715) calls all present to take up the new reality as people of God:

> Go forth into the world in peace;
> be of good courage;
> hold fast to that which is good;
> render to no one evil for evil;
> strengthen the fainthearted;
> support the weak;
> help the afflicted;
> honour all people;

love and serve God,
rejoicing in the power of the Holy Spirit.
Amen.

United Church of Christ[11]

Prayer to Mark the Anniversary of the Loss of a Loved One

God of compassion,
I remember the life of _____ that touched mine.

My heart remembers the days that were shared.
My heart remembers the love that was given.

Memories have accompanied me in this time,
Reminding me of so much received,
And so much lost.

My heart remembers the days that were shared.
My heart remembers the love that was given.

I have journeyed this path of loss,
And I have appreciated the comfort offered.

My heart remembers the days that were shared.
My heart remembers the love that was given.

My love for _____ will not be diminished.

The gifts of _____ will always remain.

My heart remembers the days that were shared.
My heart remembers the love that was given.
My heart remembers.
Amen.

Keri K. Wehlander[12]

Ritual for Endings When Strength Is Needed

You will need a supply of origami birds to do this ritual in community, or just one origami bird if you are doing this ritual on your own. Read the following:

This is a wilderness time,
when every path is obscure
and thorns have grown around words of hope.

Be the wings of strength, O God,
in this time of wilderness waiting.

This is the time of stone, not bread,
when even the sunrise feels uncertain
and everything tastes of bitterness.

Be the wings of strength, O God,
in this time of wilderness waiting.

This is the time of ashes and dust,
when darkness clothes our (my) dreams
and no star shines a guiding light.

Be the wings of strength, O God,
in this time of wilderness waiting.

This is the time of treading life,
waiting for the swells to subside
and for the chaos to clear.

Be the wings of strength, O God,
in this time of wilderness waiting.

Keri K. Wehlander[13]

My heart is in anguish within me....
And I say, "O that I had wings like a dove!
I would fly away and be at rest...."

Psalm 55:4a, 6

[B]ut those who wait for the Lord shall renew their strength,
they shall mount up with wings like eagles....

Isaiah 40:31

Pass a basket of origami birds around the group. Invite each person to take one from the basket and answer this question: What are the wings of strength you need at this time in your life?

Read the following:

Gracious Spirit,

When the dry wind of confusion
Fills our (my) every breath;
When the shadows of fear
Echo every step,
Restore our (my) heart(s) into hope
That we (I) might seek a good path.

When every door
Seems locked up tight;
When every thought
Seems weighted down,
Restore our (my) heart(s) into hope
that we (I) might seek a good path.

When the sheltering ground
Turns unstable and entangled;
When the nourishing streams
Turn hostile and arid,
Restore our (my) heart(s) into hope
That we (I) might seek a good path.
Amen.

Keri K. Wehlander[14]

Blessing Connections

Remember all the people who touched your life with shared time, love, care, comfort, and challenge, and give thanks for these people.

Prayer of Thanksgiving

For all things bright and beautiful,
For all things dark and mysterious and lovely,
For all things green and growing and strong,
For all things weak and struggling to push life up through rocky earth,
For all human faces, hearts, minds and hands which surround us,
And for all nonhuman minds and hearts, paws and claws, fins and wings,
For this life and the life of this world,
For all that you have laid before us, O God,
We lay our thankful hearts before you. In Christ's name.
Amen.

Gail Anderson Ricciuti[15]

Notes

1. *On Death and Dying: What the Dying Have to Teach Doctors, Nurses, Clergy, and Their Own Families* (New York: Simon & Schuster, 1997).
2. Catherine M. Sanders, *Surviving Grief…and Learning to Live Again.* Copyright © 1992 John Wiley & Sons, Inc. This material is used by permission of John Wiley & Sons, Inc.
3. Molly Layton, "Ripped Apart," *Psychotherapy Networker* (previously *Family Therapy Networker*) 22, no. 6 (1999): 24–31. Used by permission.
4. Copyright © 1998 Jean Vanier and the CBC. Reproduced with permission from House of Anansi Press.
5. *Caring Enough to Forgive/Caring Enough to Not Forgive* (Ventura, CA: Regal Books, 1981).
6. Stanley Keleman, *Living Your Dying*, 1975, Center Press, Berkeley, California. Used by permission.
7. *I'm Grieving as Fast as I Can: How Young Widows and Widowers Can Cope and Heal* (Far Hills, NJ: New Horizon Press, 1994).
8. *The Good Divorce: Keeping Your Family Together When Your Marriage Comes Apart*, rev. ed. (New York: HarperCollins, 1995).
9. Jack Riemer and Nathaniel Stampfer (Woodstock, VT: Jewish Lights, 1994).
10. The United Church of Canada, *Celebrate God's Presence: A Book of Services for The United Church of Canada* (Toronto: United Church Publishing House, 2000).
11. "A Service Marking the End of a Covenant." From *Book of Worship*, United Church of Christ © 1986 by United Church of Christ Office for Church Life and Leadership and reprinted © 2002 by United Church of Christ, Local Church Ministries, Worship and Education Ministry Team, Cleveland, Ohio. All rights reserved.
12. Adapted from "Our Hearts Remember" in *Circles of Grace: Worship and Prayer in the Everyday* (Toronto: United Church Publishing House, 1998), pp. 85–86. Used by permission.
13. Adapted from "Wings of Strength" in *Circles of Grace: Worship and Prayer in the Everyday* (Toronto: United Church Publishing House, 1998), pp. 95–96. Used by permission.
14. Adapted from "Wings of Strength" in *Circles of Grace: Worship and Prayer in the Everyday* (Toronto: United Church Publishing House, 1998), pp. 99–100. Used by permission.
15. Prayer by The Rev. Gail A. Ricciuti, from Gail Anderson Ricciuti and Rosemary Catalano Mitchell, *Birthings and Blessings: Liberating Worship Services for the Inclusive Church* (Crossroad, 1991). Reprinted by permission of the author.

Appendix A

The United Church of Canada: What We Believe

A New Creed

We are not alone,
*   we live in God's world.*

We believe in God:
*   who has created and is creating,*
*   who has come in Jesus,*
*   the Word made flesh,*
*   to reconcile and make new,*
*   who works in us and others*
*   by the Spirit.*

We trust in God.

We are called to be the Church:
*   to celebrate God's presence,*
*   to live with respect in Creation,*
*   to love and serve others,*
*   to seek justice and resist evil,*
*   to proclaim Jesus, crucified and risen,*
*   our judge and our hope.*
In life, in death, in life beyond death,
*   God is with us.*
We are not alone.

Thanks be to God.

Who We Are

The United Church of Canada is the largest Protestant denomination in Canada. We minister to over 3 million people in 3,820 congregations across the country. Ours is a rich history closely entwined with the development of Canada itself.

The United Church was inaugurated on June 10, 1925, in Toronto, Ontario, when the Methodist Church, Canada, the Congregational Union of Canada, and 70 percent of the Presbyterian Church in Canada entered into union. The small General Council of Union Churches, centred largely in Western Canada, joined as well. It was the first union of churches in the world to cross historical denominational lines and hence received international acclaim. Impetus for the union arose out of the concerns for serving the vast Canadian northwest and in the desire for better overseas mission. Each of the uniting churches, however, had a long history prior to 1925.

What We Believe

The doctrines of The United Church were formulated as the Basis of Union—the church's "constitution"—in 1925 and were amplified in the Statement of Faith published by the church in 1940. The United Church accepts the traditional Christian beliefs, but a wide latitude of personal interpretation is enjoyed by both lay members and professional ministers. As a result there are strongly liberal positions, ultra-conservative beliefs, and many shades in-between. The historic creeds formulated by the ancient Christian church are recognized as valuable guides to the understanding of our relationship with God. Membership is not related to the specific acceptance of a catechism or creed, but to a general acceptance of the central truths presented in the Gospel of Jesus Christ. The Bible is regarded as the wholly adequate guide or resource for the person who wants to understand Christian faith and life.

In 2003, the United Church was in the process of discussing a new Statement of Faith to reflect the new realities of our 21st-century society. At time of publication, this process was still in the consultation stage with congregations.

For more information about The United Church of Canada, visit www.united-church.ca.

Further Reading

Nurturing Relationships

Carter, Betty, with Joan K. Peters, *Love, Honor and Negotiate: Making Your Marriage Work* (New York: Pocket Books, 1997).

Family therapist Carter's cutting-edge, common-sense approach to helping marriages flourish is based on the premise that couples today want to be equals but the realities of the workplace force them into traditional roles, especially after they have children. Carter offers the best (and one of the only) discussions of the daily relational implications of a couple's financial decisions and unequal earning abilities, as well as detailed and practical discussion of transition stages.

Gottman, John M., with Nan Silver, *The Seven Principles for Making Marriage Work* (New York: Three Rivers Press, 1999).

According to most relationship books, the keys to a solid marriage are communication, communication, communication. Gottman argues that there's much more to a solid, "emotionally intelligent," marriage than efficiently sharing every feeling and thought. Through studying hundreds of couples, he offers one of the most wise, common-sense, and reassuring books available. His useable and highly regarded handbooks for couples offer in-depth quizzes, checklists, and exercises to provide the framework for coping with differences and strengthening a marriage.

————, *Why Marriages Succeed or Fail: And How You Can Make Yours Last* (New York: Fireside, 1995).

Lerner, Harriet, *The Dance of Anger: A Woman's Guide to Changing the Patterns of Intimate Relationships* (New York: HarperCollins, 1997).

A practical and wise book about anger, written for women but helpful for men as well.

————, *The Dance of Deception: A Guide to Authenticity and Truth-Telling in Women's Relationships* (New York: HarperCollins, 1994).

————, *The Dance of Intimacy: A Woman's Guide to Courageous Acts of Change in Key Relationships* (New York: HarperCollins, 1990).

Welwood, John, *Love and Awakening: Discovering the Sacred Path of Intimate Relationship* (New York: HarperPerennial, 1997).

Similar to Thomas Moore's *SoulMates* or *The Soul of Sex*, Welwood sees all relationships as opportunities to grow. His stories, exercises, and advice help readers reflect on their deepest yearnings and see how those sacred desires play in a committed lifetime relationship.

Parenting/Family Life

Barret, Robert L., and Bryan E. Robinson, *Gay Fathers: Encouraging the Hearts of Gay Dads and Their Families*, rev. ed. (San Francisco: Jossey-Bass, 2000).

New, real-life stories and up-to-date information that celebrate the power of gay fatherhood.

Doe, Mimi, and Marsha Walch, *10 Principles for Spiritual Parenting: Nurturing Your Child's Soul* (New York: HarperPerennial, 1998).

Through personal experience this book explores 10 principles to honour the spirituality of children.

Drucker, Jane, *Families of Value: Gay and Lesbian Parents and Their Children Speak Out* (New York: Insight Books, 1998).

Celebrates the joys and challenges of family life.

Hickling, Meg, *Speaking of Sex: Are You Ready to Answer the Questions Your Kids Will Ask?* (Kelowna, BC: Northstone, 1996).

Provides answers to kids' questions with current information about sexual health and sexuality.

McGinnis, James and Kathleen, *Parenting for Peace and Justice: Ten Years Later* (Maryknoll, NY: Orbis Books, 1990).

Addresses issues such as family conflict, consumerism, violence, and more from a faith-based perspective.

Nafziger, Gloria Kropf, ed., *Home Truths: Lesbian Mothers Come Out to Their Daughters* (Edmonton: Rowan Books, 2000).

Describes the changes in the mother–daughter relationship as lesbian mothers disclose their sexual orientation to their daughters.

Richardson, Ronald W., *Family Ties That Bind: A Self-Help Guide to Change through Family of Origin Therapy*, 3rd ed. (Bellingham, WA: Self-Counsel Press: 1999).

Especially useful as an accessible introduction to family systems theory, with some discussion of birth order.

Visher, Emily B., and John S. Visher, *Old Loyalties, New Ties: Therapeutic Strategies with Stepfamilies* (New York: Brunner/Mazel, 1988).

Geared more toward professionals, this book about blended families analyzes what each member brings from the old family to the new one and how the new family can be strengthened.

Same-Sex Resources

Eskridge, William N., Jr., *The Case for Same-Sex Marriage: From Sexual Liberty to Civilized Commitment* (New York: Free Press, 1996).

This more theoretical book is controversial and interesting and makes good reading in light of the resolutions on human sexuality of the United Church's 37th and 38th General Councils.

Handel, Linda, *Now That You're Out of the Closet, What about the Rest of the House?* (Cleveland, OH: Pilgrim Press, 1998).

Encouraging direction to those who have discovered that coming out is only the first step in the journey toward a fulfilling life.

Marcus, Eric, *The Male Couple's Guide: Finding a Man, Making a Home, Building a Life*, 3rd ed. (New York: HarperPerennial, 1999).

A guide for gay couples on how to build a long-lasting relationship.

Sex

Anand, Margo, *The Art of Sexual Ecstasy: The Path of Sacred Sexuality for Western Lovers* (New York: Jeremy P. Tarcher/Putnam, 1990).

A book on Eastern lovemaking for Western lovers, with a spiritual approach.

Hopkins, Jeffrey, *Sex, Orgasm and the Mind of Clear Light: The Sixty-Four Arts of Gay Male Love* (Berkeley, CA: North Atlantic Books, 1998).

A manual on tantric sex, adapted for gay men.

Love, Dr. Patricia, and Jo Robinson, *Hot Monogamy: Essential Steps to More Passionate, Intimate Lovemaking* (New York: Plume, 1994).

The best book available for long-term couples. Begins with exercises to help assess strengths and problem areas. The author breaks up "the sex thing" into such areas as romance, genital pleasure, emotional closeness, sensual loving, and so on, then provides practical exercises and specific advice to help couples address their emotional as well as sexual needs.

Muir, Charles and Caroline, *Tantra: The Art of Conscious Loving* (San Francisco: Mercury House, 1990).

An introductory book on tantric sex.

Schnarch, David, *Passionate Marriage: Sex, Love, and Intimacy in Emotionally Committed Relationships* (New York: W.W. Norton, 1997).

Schnarch's fundamental lesson is differentiation—the often threatening process of defining oneself as separate from one's partner, which inevitably draws partners closer sexually, spiritually, and emotionally.

Mid-Life

Adelman, Marcy R., ed., *Midlife Lesbian Relationships: Friends, Lovers, Children, and Parents* (New York: Harrington Park Press, 2000).

A careful and sensitive look at the various relationships of lesbians at mid-life.

Arp, David and Claudia, *The Second Half of Marriage: Facing the Eight Challenges of Every Long-Term Marriage* (Grand Rapids, MI: Zondervan, 1998).

Practical and concrete discussion of the changes and choices couples confront at key transition moments later in relationship, integrating spiritual issues into the discussion. This book is somewhat biased toward heterosexual couples with solid financial resources for retirement, but addresses basic questions many couples share.

Tindal, Mardi, *Soul Maps: A Guide to the Mid-Life Spirit* (Toronto: United Church Publishing House, 2000).

At mid-life, some things get easier and some get harder. Tindal's six chapters look at net personal worth, relationships, letting go, generational challenges, physical changes, and the blessings of mid-life. Finally, she suggests everyday practices and disciplines for nourishing the mid-life soul and contemplating the rest of one's life.

Endings

Ahrons, Constance, *The Good Divorce: Keeping Your Family Together When Your Marriage Comes Apart*, rev. ed. (New York: HarperCollins, 1995).

How couples can handle their breakup in a way that permits both adults and children to emerge as emotionally well as possible.

Augsburger, David W., *Caring Enough to Forgive/Caring Enough to Not Forgive* (Ventura, CA: Regal Books, 1981).

A Christian perspective on true forgiveness and how to repair damaged relationships.

Feinberg, Linda, *I'm Grieving as Fast as I Can: How Young Widows and Widowers Can Cope and Heal* (Far Hills, NJ: New Horizon Press, 1994).

A book especially for younger surviving spouses to help them deal with their feelings, loneliness, stress, and guilt.

Hutchison, Joyce, and Joyce Rupp, *May I Walk You Home? Courage and Comfort for Caregivers of the Very Ill* (Notre Dame, IN: Ave Maria Press, 1999).

Walking a companion home is an old-fashioned custom, a way of offering protection and guidance, and an opportunity to reflect on life and what has just been experienced. Hutchison and Rupp capture the spirit of that personal companionship for those who accompany the dying on their final journey.

Kingma, Daphne Rose, *Coming Apart: Why Relationships End and How to Live through the Ending of Yours* (Boston: Red Wheel/Weiser, 2000).

Explores why people choose partners who are wrong for them and how people can avoid repeating bad choices.

Koenig, Harold George, and Andrew J. Weaver, *Pastoral Care of Older Adults: Creative Pastoral Care and Counselling*, Creative Pastoral Care and Counselling Series (Minneapolis, MN: Fortress Press, 1998).

For the children and caregivers of older adults who face Alzheimer's disease, chronic illness, relocation, health crises, grief, depression, anxiety, gender differences, and poverty.

Layton, Molly, "Ripped Apart: What Does It Take to Turn Bitter Obsession into Forgiveness?" *Psychotherapy Networker* 22, no. 6 (1999): 24–31.

An excellent article.

Levine, Stephen, *A Year to Live: How to Live This Year as if It Were Your Last*, rev. ed. (New York: Bell Tower, 1998).

If you had only one year left to live, what would you do differently? Levine reflects on how to choose activities, relationships, and spiritual practices that reflect life's urgency rather than life's complacency. Useful for couples to work through together; includes a month-by-month program for a one-year program.

Mitsch, Raymond, and Lynn Brookside, *Grieving the Loss of Someone You Love: Daily Meditations to Help You through the Grieving Process* (Ann Arbor, MI: Vine Books, 1993).

A daily guide through grief to help people endure the anguish; understand the stages of grief; sort through the emotions of anger, guilt, fear, and depression; and face the God who allowed them to lose the people they love.

Nouwen, Henri J.M., *Our Greatest Gift: A Meditation on Dying and Caring*, rev. ed. (San Francisco: HarperSanFrancisco, 1995).

Addresses the question of how to prepare for death in a way that sends our and God's Spirit to those we have loved and who have loved us.

O'Connor, Nancy, *Letting Go with Love: The Grieving Process* (Santa Fe, NM: Mariposa Press, 1994).

A comprehensive guide to dealing with grief. Chapters include Death of Spouse, Death of Children, Death of Parents, Siblings, Friends, Death of Self, Suicide, and more.

Riemer, Jack, and Nathaniel Stampfer, eds., *So That Your Values Live On: Ethical Wills and How to Prepare Them* (Woodstock, VT: Jewish Lights, 1994).

Ethical wills try to sum up what people have learned in life and what they want most for, and from, their loved ones. While the book is written from a Jewish viewpoint, its principles can be easily adapted by people of other faiths.

Rupp, Joyce, *Praying Our Goodbyes* (Notre Dame, IN: Ave Maria Press, 1989).

This book about "the spirituality of change" is designed to help readers recognize, ritualize, reflect on, and reorient themselves in the face of loss to help heal the hurts caused by good-byes and the anxieties encountered by change, whether caused by death, loss of a job, crisis, and so on.

Sanders, Catherine M., *Surviving Grief…and Learning to Live Again* (New York: John Wiley & Sons, 1992).

As a therapist who specializes in bereavement and has experienced significant personal loss, Sanders sets out some of the common experiences or phases everyone goes through in dealing with grief.

Vaughan, Diane, *Uncoupling: Turning Points in Intimate Relationships* (Cary, NY: Oxford University Press, 1986).

Based on 10 years' research and interviews with straight and gay couples, married and live-in, this carefully documented book shows how couples come apart.

Videos and Feature Films

Better Than Chocolate (Trimark, 1999). 101 minutes.

A sympathetic and often hilarious depiction of heterosexual, lesbian, bisexual, and transgendered couples and individuals.

Kramer vs. Kramer (Columbia Tri-Star, 1979). 105 minutes.

Though older, this movie remains relevant in its exploration of the failure of marriage and the often stressful shift of parental roles.

The Story of Us (Universal, 1998). 94 minutes.

A great conversation-starter: People either love or hate this video as it explores what blows a marriage apart and what keeps it together.

When a Man Loves a Woman (Touchstone, 1994). 125 minutes.

Another good conversation-starter. A couple in a long-term marriage begins to realize how much of a role alcohol has played in bringing them together in the first place, in their marriage, and now in serious alcoholism. The genuinely good-hearted husband comes to realize that what looks like his wife's problem will require difficult changes in both of them.

When Night Is Falling (Hallmark, 1995). 94 minutes.

A Canadian film about two women discovering each other.

Web Sites

Visit the "Marriage and Life Partnership" pages of The United Church of Canada's Web site: www.united-church.ca/marriage.

Catholic Engaged Encounter: www.engagedencounter.org.

This organization provides weekend marriage preparation workshops mainly for Catholic couples, but non-Catholics are welcome.

Enrich Canada: www.empoweringcouples.ca.

This organization provides marriage preparation and enrichment programs.

Good for Her: www.goodforher.com.

A woman-friendly Canadian store of adult books, videos, and sex toys that celebrates women's sexuality.

Jewish Marriage Encounter: www.jewishmarriage.org.

This organization provides weekend marriage enrichment workshops for couples.

United Worldwide Marriage Encounter: www.uwwme.org.

UWWME is entirely led by volunteer members, both clergy and lay, of The United Church of Canada.

United Worldwide Marriage Enrichment: www.gbgm-umc.org/me-incOH/welcome.htm.

This non-denominational Christian organization runs marriage enrichment workshops.

The Vanier Institute of the Family: www.vifamily.ca.

The Vanier Institute promotes the importance of families in Canada and studies the challenges they face. A primarily education- and research-based Web site.